Introduction

WINGS *of* FREEDOM: Poems of Victory and Inspiration was developed from a broken heart needing to mend. This book was written for the readers to connect to their life force, God, through any adversity, obstacle or situation. These poems are meant to stir the soul and bring deep emotions to the surface of our lives to heal us. These poems will evoke the soul and penetrate the core. This book is meant to free our innermost feeling about joy, sorrow, love, hatred, peace, anger, happiness, frustrations and hope for a brighter future of freedom to believe.

Rev. date: 06/24/2013

To order additional copies of this book, contact:
Xlibris Corporation
1-888-795-4274
www.Xlibris.com
Orders@Xlibris.com

WINGS

of

FREEDOM

ANITA N. SAVAGE

To my courageous and precious special gifts, Ariel, Miles and Malachi;

my patient and strong parents, Theodore and Marguerite Savage;

my supportive and encouraging sister and brother-in-law,

Dr. Angela Savage-Davis and Roger Davis;

my steadfast and wise brother, Teddy Savage.

I love you all for everything you are to me and all the

inspiration you've given me on this journey

Table of Contents

In Between the Crack

In between the cracks of love.
In between the cracks of pain.
In between the cracks of the remains,
That no one could ever really.
But I know!
The cracks only are made to be filled,
Made to heal,
Made to be completely sealed.
The cracks are made to help us grow.
The cracks are made to help us know
That the pain of love
Will never really stop
That rose from growing in between that rock.
So when you think of
Down and out,
Think of all the times

When you climbed out the crack
And you looked at your life
And you said, "Hey! I'm on top!"
So just remember the TOP ain't that far
Because that crack ain't that deep
And if you look at yo'self
You'll know
That you can…
Reach up and grab
The top of that crack.
And baby, baby, baby
You'll never look back!
Because when the crack is sealed,
And the time is healed
You'll know that HE is real!

Heavenly Name

Heavenly is the name
That sets my soul free.
Heavenly is that name
For the entire world to see and believe.
For his spirit flows,
Like the dove in flight
Gliding against the wind
Fighting to keep balance.
And when that spirit flows and soars
above all else,
Even heaven's angels have to catch their
breath.
In awe of that name, He has come to reclaim
This sinful world and cleanse our souls.
I believe that his name is so heavenly
That my soul rejoices.
When I hear the breeze whisperin' in my ears,

When I see the rose so sweet,
Bloomin' in May,
When I hear my children play,
When I see that maternal love, so strong
From above.
Cause' when Mary laid

Sweet Jesus down
And never asked for reasons why,
She was the one to have his son.
Cause' his love is everlasting even in the
Silence of his birth
The heavens praised in full rejoice
That all the earth would soon proclaim,
The purity that God has given for all who remain
For his name is holy here below and on high.
That heavenly name.

Mirror Image

What do you see when you look at
Yourself in the mirror?
What looks back at you?
Is it joy?
Is it pain?
Is it love?
Is it shame?
When I look in the mirror, you
Know what I see?
I see hope…
Hope for me to be
All that I can be.
Hope for me to see
Dreams that I can't see.
But you know
God's love for me was that he made me
In the IMAGE that I see.
God touched me
And he breathed life in me.
So deeply, that I see!
But I had to see through all of that pain,
I had to see through all of that frustration.

In those times when I didn't know
Where I would go.
But now that I see you look just like me.
Because through those eyes that I see
I see a mirror IMAGE of me.
Because the life that I live,
The troubles that I face the devil
Cannot try to erase,
That IMAGE that God gave me.
So keep tryin' devil
All that you want!
Cause you know what God's got my back!
And you know what?
The IMAGE that I see
Can beat you,
Defeat you,
Stomp you into nothing!
Because that mirror that God's given me to see
Through is holy, divinely blessed
Because that mirror IMAGE
Is God's holy grace!

Soul (sole) Mate

If you look at the bottom of your shoe, there's a sole.
Nice and hard, rubber or slippery, high or cushiony,
or comfortable
Why do I talk about the sole of a shoe and how it
relates to the soul mate?
Ponder that question in your mind.
The sole of your shoe gives you support
Does it not?
Does it keep your feet dry?
Does it give you the lift that you need to feel higher
in height?
Does it make you feel sexy and important
In times of stress?
Does it make you feel like you're home at last?
Ready to take on that day with confidence?
Ready to play or exercise?
And when it comes to a soul mate,

Do not they bring you that same joy?
Should they not give you that place of comfort in times
of trials?
Should they not give you hope?
That if I keep steppin' and pushin' toward the mark
That one day I will feel whole because the soul
Is where we find support.

Yes, my soul mate SHOULD SUPPORT MY SOUL!
In that they should keep me safe make me feel at home.
So a soul mate doth exist because you do have a soul.
So when you need some advice.
Look at the bottom of your shoe
And think, do not I continue to step!
So soul mate here I come!
Soul mate here I be!
Soul mate get ready for me!

Stomp

Satan tries to
Manipulate and possess you.
Because he knew you were weak.
Why is weakness vulnerability?
Why can't weakness be Strength?
In strength we find God!
God is our only weapon,
Our only weapon,
Against that Satan
That we call friend.
That Satan that wants us to be his friend.
What really are we doing
when Satan is in?
We cannot heal.
We cannot feel.
We cannot go beyond our limited minds.

Because Satan is your friend.
Friends come and friends go.
But friends never sell you real low like Satan
His name means deceiver,
His name means manipulator
His name is UGLY!
So why do we call his name like he's a friend

He ain't nobody that can make you whole.
He is a demon, ready to devour your soul
So people, STOMP that devil out!
Stomp so you can release the doubt
That God is real!
Stomp, my people
Stomp!

I Feel You

I feel you like the oceans
Feel the moon.
When the tide comes and hits the coast line
I feel you.
I feel you with the warmth of a nice blanket
On a cold winter's night.
I feel you
When the sun peaks over that pike.
And when I feel you
I look at you and I see
God's done it all for me.
And when I look at you
I see all of the ways in which love can be expressed.
Thru a gentle touch
Thru a sweet kiss.
Love exists,
If only we feel each other.
So when I feel you like cashmere on the skin so soft.
I feel the love that He has placed in your heart.
So don't ever stop thinking that I never feel you
Cause I know, as long as my heart beats that warm
blood through my veins

Nothing, nothing can stop that feeling
That I feel when I look at you.
I see the light,
That warmth, that light that creates all beings
That lives in all of us.
That light it shines so bright
And when I look at you
I feel you.
I feel that energy from within
I feel that energy that no one can destroy.
That energy that lasts beyond this lifetime
and more,
That energy that gives all life a meaning.
Give me that energy so that I can keep it close
to my heart.
Cause' I know that energy gives me peace and harmony.
I need to feel you, so that you can feel me.
And in that time that we feel one another
You'll know that it will last forever.

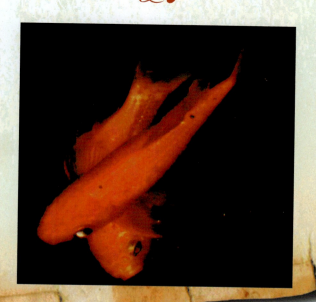

Jubilee

All the love
That we can see
Jubilee is deep inside of me.
But what is it that I feel
When jubilee hits me?
I feel free.
I feel peace.
I feel harmony.
I feel like me!
Trapped up inside is a sense of confidence.
I'm confident enough to stand against the ways
of the world.

I'm confident enough to be that soldier at the end of
the road.
Looking down at the valley below,
Thinking the jubilation within came because
I was patient!
I was jubilant!
When I knew those times of pain and sorrow
It just helped me to grow
Now I know jubilation is my friend
It doesn't matter when.
But jubilation is found within.

Butterfly...Is that you?

Butterfly… is that you?

Butterfly…I can't feel blue looking at you.

Flapping your wings against the breeze, so light,

Light as a feather floating through the air.

You pretty butterfly.

You have been blown here

You have been blown there.

Butterfly, how can I feel you from way over there?

Yea… It must be the butterfly effect that changes the way we met.

Because the innocence of your flight; so unique and it feels so right.

Butterfly have we known each other before?

Because it seems that we've reached a place

Where if you didn't exist over there,

How could I be here?

Looking around trying to wonder why I see what I've already known.

Butterfly that's my home!

Being a butterfly so free!

Hey! That's what I been missing being me!

Flying so high that no one can hold me down,

And you feel me when I'm around.

I'm around to change your world.

I'm around because of the knowledge of self!

To metamorphosize into what your purpose is to be is to be mighty like the softest wings of that little butterfly.

Because you see when that little butterfly's wings flapped,

As it flaps

It changes the tides

It changes the climate.

So that's got to be it!

Because the metamorphosis that I took

It took me awhile to see that I'm a different me!

And I'm more beautiful than before.

When I was crawling up into that cocoon,

Ready to rest and reflect

And sleep.

In my mental state to know

As time goes on, I must grow.

And when I do what emerges from that cocoon

Is who I truly am!

On the inside and out

That beautiful wing span that God gave me to

Expand my mind to know that

I can soar higher than that branch that I use to crawl upon.

I can soar much higher than that ground that kept me before.

Now my skies are limitless

because of my METAMORPHOSIS!

Sistah Souljah

Sistah souljah, there's no other like
Sistah souljah.
Marching down that dreary lane
Trying to refrain.
Refrain from the enigma
Of the o' so clever way, the world tries to eradicate
Your edifice
And the magnificence
Of the feminine qualities
That dwells from your creativity.
Sistah souljah,
God's creation of youthfulness
Of kindness
Effortlessly feminine.
Sistah souljah,
Your breastplate is as strong as
The way that you contemplate; the battlefield of
all creation.
There is no compensation for our sacrificial lives.
Sacrificing for our children,
Sacrificing for our men.
We got it all inside

But we can't keep it in.
We can keep it in no more
Sistah souljah!
It's time to fight the good fight!
Time to ignite the people
Give them back
What God gave to us!
Give them back their motivation,
The sensation of authority.
We need the quality
Of your femininity
To produce souljahs from mothers.
These souljahs will fight

For the right
To survive.
In God's own time will we know what they are
needed for.
No more can we sit and wait,
No more can we contemplate,
How life tries to devastate
Our children, our men
Souljah it's time to begin!

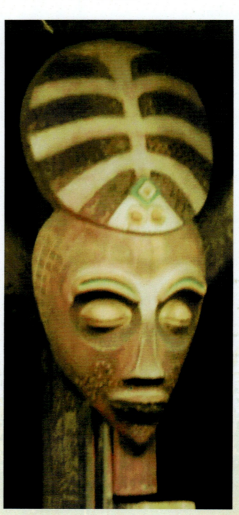

Infinity

If infinity could be spoken in one word
What would you think it would be?
Like the single drop of the morning dew
Infinity=consistency.
Therefore life has the ability to provide unity.
Unity between the body and soul
Entirely conforming to be one's own consulate.
Yet the desolation of the unknown, the ignorance
of bliss.
That actually gives us the ability
To feel infinity.
So don't be afraid
To cross the plane
Because when your time has come
Throughout that journey,
That we all must take
We need to reach
Deep inside to know that infinity is prosperity.

The prosperity of you
To expand for life
Into the next level

Knowing that when we cross into the unknown realm
of spirituality
The infinity of our spirituality is definitely God's grace.
His ultimate sacrifice to show us that infinity
is consistency.
Being consistent in your praise,
Being consistent in your love
Being consistent in your knowledge
To obtain all that life has to give.
Because when we cross into the infinite
All we will have is the wisdom gained embedded in
our spirit.
So be free,
In your spirituality because in it is infinity.

Intimacy

Do you know what love is?

Do you know the course of my heart?

Wait a minute you're going the wrong way.

My heart lies deeper the touch that you give me in that way.

You're going in the wrong direction!

It has nothing to do with an erection!

It has nothing to do with the conception

Of the way my curves glide across my body

That's not what I speak of.

Intimacy must be dealt with gently

It must be seen in secrecy,

In privacy.

Because in love we touch places that no one can see

Except for the one above

He knows the true sense of love

He knows the true sense of intimacy.

So why is it so hard for you to conceive

Not even touching me?

For me to feel that love that permeates within goes farther than the touch of the skin.

So don't look at me as if you don't know what I

Mean when I say, "Stop playin'!"

"Stopin' with your role

Stop playin' for what you know;

That touch only lasts for a minute."

But the intimacy that I speak of comes straight from above.

The only way to tap that is: give me a piece of your secrecy.

The secrecy of your moments in silence,

When you tap in that space

That no one can erase.

That internal you that beams, when all that it seem to be you

Lies from a place of pureness, innocence and confidence.

To love someone is to nurture the one thing

That no one can see

That is intimacy.

So don't go on thinking about the sexual pleasure

That desire for the flesh.

I can deal with more of the internal bliss

And nothing less.

So stroke my ego as you might say

For the ego that makes me will never go away

So don't think that I'm arrogant when I say

That God gave me something not for just any man could please.

God gave it to me for only one man to see

So when the time comes,

And I'm ready to grow

In my intimacy;

The whole world will know.

Bloom

When the time comes for you to bloom
You'll know that you always had room.
Room to grow,
Room to show
That the love would always let you know.
Know that the time it takes you to be
It was easy to see.
That the only thing that was stopping you
From blooming
Was consuming
The trueness of his omnipotence.
He's always there with us.
Waiting for the time

To give us that
Joy, peace and courage to bloom.
So now it is time for you
To push through that soil.
Uncoil your love.
Uncoil your pain.
Uncoil your sense of awareness.
Because as time goes on
That bud most bloom.

And when it blooms,
Don't allow anything to consume
That joy that grows from within.

Why Not?

Take your own journey.

Pick you own place to go.

Ride your own train.

Who cares where you go.

But why not go with a new life in your step?

Why not go with a new joy in your heart?

There's got to be a change.

It's as if we took that step,

Stepping into the darkness

Not knowing if the light was going to be there.

Walking through that dark tunnel

Can't see front and in back.

But somehow we couldn't lack

The knowledge that everything has it's time and place.

So it doesn't matter where you're going

What part of the race you're on,

It's time to reach for the light,

Even if it's out of sight.

Because that is believing,

That is trusting.

We can move through the darkness together

Because we are forever.

We are eternally

Apart of the bond

That created the entire universe.

Just think as you walk through that darkness.

Just think as you walk,

Every step that you take

Is getting you a little closer to the light of tomorrow,

Where there is no more sorrow.

No more pain!

The rain… cannot stop

The flood of the full rejoice!

Soon we all will see!

You will be a part of the essence of the eternity!

Because once we receive;

There's no more left

But to believe that which you can only conceive.

So take that journey with me

And the light will be your epiphany.

Rise Up

History tell us
That our identity was stripped,
Our humanity was questioned.
But you see they did us a favor
By selecting the best qualities;
In preparation for our victories.
It didn't take us long to realize
That as people we will rise!
I know that the times
Seem unbearable,
But the time of change
Are inevitable.
So brothas and sistahs
The plan is this…
We will rise again
Right now!

We must insist that
We don't allow what you see
To manipulate all the possibilities of our destinies.
Our children will rise as leaders of tomorrow.
We must be an example for them to follow,
So stop selling yourselves for the almighty dollar.

In the end will devour
Your soul, your mind, your being whole
And spit you out like yesterdays trash!
Let's change our mentality so that we will last!
No more waiting in the wind
Brothas and sistahs
We will win!
But we have to take a stand.

Greatness is Knocking

Greatness is something
I know we all have.
If only we were able to release and unify.
Unify, we must come together as one.
No matter where we are,
No matter what place you are on your journey.
It's time to be free!
Young and old,
Rich and poor,
Black, white, gay, or straight.
When it all comes down to it
Greatness has no face
It's a spirit.
The spirit that leads the world to greatness!
Don't be afraid to feel
That spirit!
As powerful as it is
It can defeat the darkness!
Because with greatness comes love,
Love of self

Love of your brother and sister.
Our children
Deserve to feel that spirit of greatness.

That's why we're here
Because of people that have stepped out
And took it upon themselves to show others greatness.
I'm not afraid anymore
because greatness is knocking at my door!
I'm not afraid not to know what to say;
Love always find a way.
So if greatness is knocking at your door
You can't stop it anymore.
You can't sleep at night.
The time is right!
When your greatness is discovered
History is being made
Because change has come!
We can no longer run!

Harriet Tubman
1820-1913

Frederick Douglass
1817-1895

Sojourner Truth
1797-1883

Prelude to Greatness is Knocking

Greatness is something
That is inspired
At any stage
In anyone's life.
There's no one time
And no one age
That we can acquire greatness.
Greatness is something that blooms;
When your back is against the wall.
And there's no other place to go
Or you will fall.
Our ancestors fought
For something that we feel on the inside.
It's wrapped up in the those thoughts of insecurity

And false identity.
If we are to acquire greatness
We have to be able to push aside our fears.
The fears of failure,
The fears of hardship,
The fears of pain.
If our struggles is to mean something
We have to push past

We have to settle for nothing less than greatness.
I just imagine the courage that it took for
A whole nation to accept every man as his brother;
And we struggle to stop judging one another.
Greatness is something clever!

In the Middle

I fit right in the middle.
A little girl, pigtails and big grin.
I knew no idea of sin.
Jumpin', skippin', hopscotch
Jump ropin' playin', back n forth
Sayin', "Hey I was that little middle class girl!"
Livin' right in between fantasy and reality!
Growin', blossomin', appreciatin'
The best of both worlds.
G.G. and great-grand mommy
Fillin' my tummy
With the sweetest candies!
Lovin' house that was glowin'
From the inside out.
Everything about it made me feel good, loved,
cherished, needed and wanted.
And I was meant to be.
Mum-mum the other side of the dirt road
Where it was just as much fun!
Giggling' and whisperin'
Hidin', tryin' not to have Mum-mum listen

But she could hear everything
We always wondered, as we were playin'.
Family, food, music and the stoop that never

Grew old, and it lasted forever.
Swingin', glidin', watchin' the day go by
Eatin' corner store onion pickles,
As our lips puckered from the sourness of our treat.
The corner store had it all.
All my friends dusty and dirty
Playin' with me.
It didn't matter that I was livin' in the middle
Of fantasy and reality.
Back then we didn't care.
All we wanted was to be friends.
Laughin' was our medicine.
As time went on the feelings just grew stronger.
Our childhood dreams began to wonder,
But we still remember the love we shared
On those long days that we played
In the middle.

Time to Heal

Time to heal.
Healing, revealing, the inner most parts.
Trying, concealing, faking
Frustrating, confusing, self manipulation.
Confession,
Healing, mending
Transcending the pain
Of the layers that no longer have a hold on me.
The hardest thing I ever had to be
Was the real me!
Never compromising the trueness
Of the realest part of me.
It's time for the sun to set
It's time for me to forget
All of those painful sources

Of my torment!
But I don't regret
All those sunsets.
They helped me to heal.
The time has come
For the sun to rise.
Time to realize
If only I could've shed those layers

Maybe you could've seen the healing.
No time to look back
At the impact of this healing process.
The flawless, timeless
Healing process.

Eternally Somebody

Knowing you're something
When you have all the opportunities to exist.
Wanting to be something
That we knew could be SIMPLY.
And as we grow in the simple grace
Of his divine touch.
Blessing us continuously.
In as much as time moves
Our world,
The sun rises and falls.
In the presence of it all
Is the touch
That created this somebody.
When you place your hand
On your heart
And feel the rhythmic beats
We cannot stand apart
From the divine presence
That uplifts our souls.

That gives up permission to feel;
Simplicity in the meekness of the soul.

When it has time to expose
Our innermost strengths.
We all will be able to see
That we always been somebody!
Nothing comes from nothing!
Your existence is a matter of consciousness.
Being fully present
In the omnipotence of the divine touch
That held us so close
In the mere darkness
Of our existence.
Because out of that darkness,
He created the light.
The light that creates every life force in
The universe
And we are eternally somebody.

Golden Years

The look of achievement is on your face.
The look of wisdom and grace
Shines all around you
With every simple, beautiful glimpse.
A glimpse of the past in which you stepped
And left your footprint.
Even though times that you've wept;
Wept for the generations that came after,
Wept for the present
Of the coming after.
After all that is said and done
We still rise and become the ones.
The ones that have risen above
And were able to strive
To lift and be
The golden you to help me.
There's times when I wonder,

"Will I ever reach those years?"
Fighting away the tears.
Knowing that if I exist
Then I will reach those golden years.
In those golden years you were able to
Experience the laughter, love, joy, and pain.

But we still remain… GOLDEN!
So shine on my queens
For this is your day
A day to shine the brightest ever!
We cherish you forever!
Golden years
Are my goal
Because I know in the end
They will make me whole.

What you Looking At?

You lookin' at me?
Wonder why that is?
Yea, I'm talkin' to you!
You think you know who I am?
Please!
The sleekness of my frame
You wish you could touch
The vastness of my brain.
It's alright
A lot of guys don't really get it.
You know why?
Because they are so limited
To what they think they know me,
About my femininity.
Please!
All I want you to do
Is to take a minute
To step outside of your ego.
Look into reality
And tell me what you really see.
If you really wanted to
Answer the question

You don't have to say anything
Or the way you think
I may be.
I'm not interested
In the physical sense
Of your meager explanation
About what you think about me.
I see you watching me
Wondering what you could do or see
I was never able to see past the physical myself.
Because no one really
Knew the value of my wealth;
And that's okay too.
Cause as long as I live

I'm good just being me.
So keep looking, keep dreaming, keep staring.
I've given too much away.
I'm never going there again.
I'm here to stay.
You might try to manipulate what you think is true.
All I want is a friend
To talk to, confide in, believe in.

Somebody that can caress my pain away
With the sweetest touch.
Someone that can pray with me.
Strengthen my soul
When all is lost
And hope is low
I want my friend to love me from within
So you can keep walking.

Shackled

Shackled by our burdens.
Shackled by our fears.
I know as time goes on
We become torn and worn.
We forgot how long it took
For us to believe
That we could be strong
Enough to release
Those shackles.
How long will it take
For you to recognize your worth?
The shackles may not be physical
But I know you feel them just the same.
As long as you are here
The shackles will try to bind you.
Don't bind yourself with mediocrity.
Don't bind yourself in a position of inferiority,
As if you are minuscule
To the way the world visualizes you.
If we all carried those

Shackles, all our lives;
As our ancestors once did, all their lives,
We will be lost.

How can we elevate
To another level of consciousness?
We know what is true about us
How dare we settle for shackles!
I'm tired of carrying these shackles!
I'm tired of living those someone else's eyes!
I'm tired of being someone else's prize!
I'm tired of being someone else's toys!
I'm tired of being someone else's ploy!
In the game of life
Put down, release, undue your shackles.
Whether you believe it or not
You are in bondage until you make it.
I refuse to settle for anything less
I will challenge myself and achieve the best!
So please put the shackles down now!

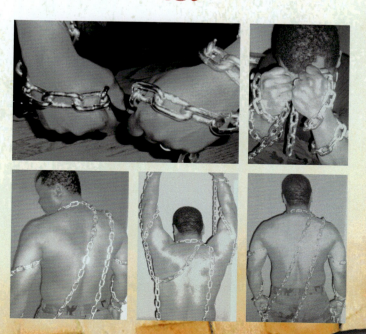

Wet Nurse

As you suckle the little ones
And provide nourishment;
With all the time spent
You are their essence.
If I took all that you have given
And wrapped it up in
The sweetest way
It would take a million years to say,
"How grateful for the energy you've expended."
We never knew your strength.
We know that all of us were provided with that love.
In the darkest time that we felt so lost.
But you planted the seed.
The seed for us to know we are loved.
Without you that position would've have been filled.
We might not have belonged to you,
But you gave so much and it made us

Feel brand new.
But as we grew
And massa' told us what to do
We still knew in the back
Of our subconscious

That God loved us.
Because the sweetest milk
That gave us life
Could've have been enough for us to make it
Through the strife.
If we didn't believe that we meant something
Or had so much to give
No matter how much time we had
We were yours,
Enough said!

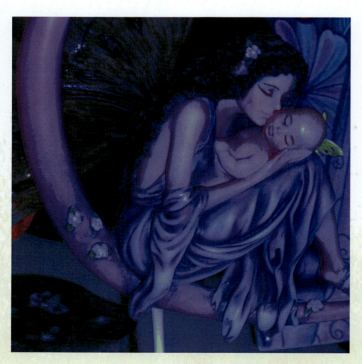

Challenges

Broken promises
All kinds of excuses
Why you feel useless.
The mundane, chaotic, intense
Events that occur over and over again.
And the challenges to left and right
Feeling defenseless
Against these challenges.
Nevertheless hope rests buried beneath
These challenges.
Sometimes I wonder,

Why God choose me to deal with
These challenges?
The only answer is: I'm destined to be more than a
conqueror!
Destined to rise above
These challenges!
Don't look at me with pity or shame
Because even though I might complain.
My life wouldn't be the same without
These challenges.

Out There

Out there beyond the clouds
Entranced in the fusion
Of the chasmic calamity.
The chaos of the minute effects
Which were affected by the cause.
The cause out there
The placement of its dimensions
Out there.
Close enough to see,
Yet far enough not to touch.
The overwhelming effect is evident.
Because of the way our bodies vibrate
When we touch.

The effects of how incredible
It feels when we feel the inevitable.
As we search for the answers
Out there.
The question still lies:
How are we connected and comprised?
How often do we think about:
 Why we are here at all?

Don't get caught up in the cause
Because after all the EFFECT is…
Out there?

It Is Well

It is well with my soul.
All that I know,
All that I feel
Is so real.
It's okay to not know
Where the next step is going to lead.
It's okay to not be all
That you want to be or need.
But the soul is the source of comfort.
It is well with my soul!
When all else seems unsure
My soul knows that I'm pure.
I will not allow the chaos of this world
To bring me to a place of indignation or shame
Because my soul is the purest connection
 To my destination.
That destination might not seem real when
The times get rough,
But in time we will see that
We always were enough.
We always were able to be
That which we couldn't see
It's time to be trustworthy

It's time to be free!
Cause when all else fails
It is well with our souls.
Seems easier said than done
But I would rather live in joy,
Then live in shame or pain.
So when I look around and I see nothing
That I'm happy or joyous about
I don't have any doubts
Because my soul is well.
So not a cloud in the sky
Or no kind of rain can wash away
That feeling that allows
Me to be
So keep on believing that
In order for you to go through
This temporary wasteland
You must get to the core of your spirit.
That's the ticket
To a place of pure ecstasy,
Blatantly, dynamically, joyfully my commitment
To live for eternity.

Fading Away

At times I feel that it's easy
Easy to place my hands on what I can see
But as I began to realize that
The image is always
Fading away.
Fading away without a care
Were you ever really there?
Is the question that needs to be asked because
My heart is so fragile
And I can't take it if you
Left me standing here.
When you leave, all I do
Is think of the goodness
That I must breathe in.
In order to mend
Those secret places
That only you and I know.
So please don't go
Please stay for a little while longer,
So that this image can linger inside my soul.
I need your touch.
I need your kiss.
The simple bliss

Of those intimate pleasures.
But you see fading away
Might be all that we have left;

In order to keep it strong.
Because I know
How much I long
For the time that we have;
The time that we had.
And as I grow more into who I am,
I'm starting to see
That presence has helped me to love again.
And to be that sweet, sweet spirit
That you held so close for so long.
The innocence of my love for you
Cannot be spoken in words.
But I know that even if I touch the intangible
Parts of you,
Well then fading away
Would blend us and create something new
That we can hold on to.
Something that we can rely on when we're feeling blue.
Because as I go on I'll know that
When you did fade away into my dreams,
Seems as though you've left your imprint
Of the softest, timeless love.
So fade away if you must
But remember as long as I live,
As long as God gives me air in my lungs.
You will never ever fade away for too long.

Is That All You See

Is that all you see?
The insane controversy
Of the lack of humanity.
Because you see when you look at me
You only can see
With your close minded eyes.
That fills the void
Of the consciousness,
Of discrimination;
The resurrection of the times.
Past, present and future
Full of peoples' thoughts that twirl
In the reverse
Of what we use to traverse.
Time to be
Confused, by the way
That you look at me?
Destined for the darkness
Because of the calamity
Of the mystery.
In worrying about
The dark skin of me

Is that all you see?
Is that really all
You see when you look at me?
The brown tones of my melanin?
Because if you really
Took the time to have a conversation,
You will discover that skin
Is only the beginning.
The beginning of the story
That's meant to be told.
Beginning of the chapter
That's yet to unfold.
Because when we come together

Without looking, without seeing the outside,
That's when God will provide the lessons
For us to learn.
If we're only one race
Full of his grace
Then it's time to shine
Because if not now, then we're destined
To die.

Die in the misery
Of our shame.
Because we never could look past?
We never could try to see past?
The eye of discrimination
Stereotypically imperfectedly human?
Because we only should see
That the color of the skin
Is just the beginning
And not the end.

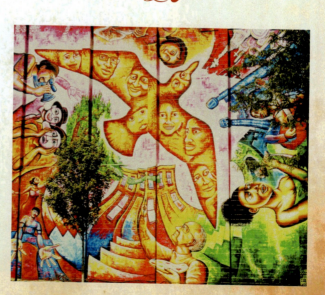

Faithful

Faithfulness is a place of dignity,
A place of oneness
And trueness,
To one's own promises,
To one's own self.
So why is it that faithfulness
Does not come without a price?
We have to sell ourselves short,
We have to look at ourselves in shame.
And then we have to remember
All that pain,
All the strife,
That we created in our own life.
And then when we look at faithfulness
As if it's something that doesn't quite exist.
Because in this time…
We can't even STOP!
And just admire what God has given us.
Because faithfulness

Is something that is hard to do
For your own self.
But how much lack of love
Do we have?
That we can't even give ourselves love?
I don't have time to look at myself
In the mirror,
And feel honored to be in the skin
That GOD gave me?
Faithfulness
Is something that is achieved.
Because when we look at life
And we look at everything we've done
Faithfulness
Is what brought us through.
So how about you,
Stop looking at yourself feeling sorry
And start looking at yourself with dignity
Because faithfulness is all we need.

Raindrops

Every drip drop of my misery.
Every fallen dream.
Every time the rain drops fall,
They always seem to cleanse my soul.
Regardless of the way I feel
As the rain drips down
I know that it heals.
I know that as I am submerged in my sadness.
The more that the rain falls
Covering the madness.
I know that once
The rain stops dripping from me,
Then the sun will beam.
The sun will gleam.
It's beautiful light on me
So that I can see;
See the purity
Of the crystal clear simplicity.
The smallest raindrops on me.
So let it rain,
Let it pour,
So that I don't have to feel

That hurt anymore.
I'll soak my clothes,

Cause all I want to do
Is to dispose
All those
Wasted thoughts.
The manipulated actions,
False reactions
Of those shallow infractions
Of my mind.
Cause the rain drops
Slower in time,
So that I can actually
Dry my eyes.
But I can't do it by myself
So God please send the rain
Because you know
The places that are stained.
You know the time
It takes to mend those scars
Deep within
So let all the rain drip
Drop from my skin
For in the end
I will be pure again.

Printed in the United States
by Baker & Taylor Publisher Services